CAN'T I JUST SKIP COLLEGE?
For Everyone Who Closed the First Book and Still Didn't Want a Dorm Room

Jennifer Larsen

A Wayfinder Series Companion for the No-College Path

Originality Statement

This book is an original work written by the author and reflects their unique ideas, voice, and instructional approach. While it may reference common educational and career-planning concepts, all content, including structure, language, exercises, and framework, is the author's own creation. Any similarities to other published works are purely coincidental.

Printed in the United States of America

First Edition

Cover design by Rachel Bostwick

Interior design and layout by Rachel Bostwick

CAN'T I JUST SKIP COLLEGE?
For Everyone Who Closed the First Book and Still Didn't Want a Dorm Room

📖 Introduction: Success Without College

For as long as you can remember, you've probably been told that college is **the** path to success. Teachers, parents, and society push the idea that **a degree equals a good job, stability, and a better life.** And for some people, that's true.

But what if college **isn't** the right fit for you? What if the idea of spending four (or more) years in a classroom, taking on tens of thousands of dollars in debt, doesn't sound like the best way to start your life?

Here's the truth: **College is just one path—not the only path.** There are **high-paying careers, fulfilling jobs, and entrepreneurial opportunities** that don't require a degree. And choosing to skip college now **doesn't mean you can't go later.** It just means you're taking a different approach—one that gets you earning money faster and avoids student debt while still keeping your future open.

What This Book Will Help You Do

This book is your **guide to success without a degree.** It will show you:

- **Careers that don't require college** but still pay well and have room for growth.
- **Entrepreneurial and freelancing options** if you'd rather work for yourself.
- **Alternative education paths** that don't cost a fortune.
- **How to get hired without a degree** and stand out in the job market.
- **How to build long-term career success** even without a diploma.
- **The financial advantages** of skipping or delaying college—and how to make your money work for you.

This book **isn't anti-college**—it's **pro-options.** If you ever decide you need a degree down the line (for management roles, career shifts, or personal goals), you can always pursue it **on your own terms.** But if you're looking for a way to start a **successful career now, without spending years in school,** this book will show you exactly how to do it.

🎯 **Let's get started.**

📖 Section 1:
High-Paying Careers Without a Degree

When most people think of high-paying jobs, they assume a college degree is required. But that's **not** the case. There are **plenty of well-paying careers** that don't require four years of school—many of which let you start earning money much faster than your college-bound peers.

In this section, we'll explore some of the best career options that don't require a degree, including:

- **Skilled Trades** – Jobs that build and repair the world around us

- **Tech Careers** – High-paying digital and IT jobs with certifications instead of degrees

- **Public Service & First Responders** – Stable careers with strong benefits

- **Medical Careers Without a Degree** – Essential roles in healthcare that don't require a four-year diploma

- **Manufacturing & Logistics** – High-demand jobs that keep industries running

- **High-Value Sales** – A lucrative field where **your skills matter more than your education**

Let's break down these paths and how you can get started.

Skilled Trades: Building, Fixing, and Keeping the World Running

Skilled trades are some of the most **secure, high-paying, and in-demand** careers out there. These are jobs that **can't be outsourced—** someone **has** to install electrical wiring, repair HVAC systems, or build houses **right here.**

🔧 **Examples of Skilled Trades:**

- ✔ **Electricians** ($50K–$90K+ per year)

- ✔ **Plumbers** ($50K–$100K+ per year)

- ✔ **HVAC Technicians** ($45K–$80K per year)

- ✔ **Welders & Fabricators** ($40K–$85K per year)

- ✔ **Carpenters** ($45K–$80K per year)

- ✔ **Heavy Equipment Operators** ($50K–$95K per year)

💲 **Why Choose This Path?**

- ☑ **Earn while you learn** – Many trades offer **paid apprenticeships**, meaning you get paid **while training.**

- ☑ **No student loan debt** – Trade schools cost a fraction of college tuition.

- ☑ **High demand & job security** – Trades are always needed, and demand is growing.

- ☑ **Growth potential** – Start as an apprentice, become a journeyman, and later open your own business.

🚀 **How to Get Started:**

- ✔ Look for **apprenticeship programs** in your area (often found through unions or trade schools).

✔ Consider a **trade school** (usually 6 months to 2 years).

✔ **Start as an entry-level helper** and gain hands-on experience.

Tech Careers: High-Paying Jobs Without a Degree

Tech jobs aren't just for people with computer science degrees. Many **high-paying tech careers** can be started with **certifications, bootcamps, or self-taught skills.**

💻 **Examples of Tech Careers:**

- ✔ **IT Support Specialist** ($40K–$75K per year)

- ✔ **Web Developer** ($50K–$100K per year)

- ✔ **Cybersecurity Analyst** ($60K–$120K per year)

- ✔ **Digital Marketer** ($50K–$100K per year)

- ✔ **Data Analyst** ($55K–$110K per year)

💰 **Why Choose This Path?**

- ☑ **Many jobs focus on skills, not degrees** – Companies hire based on what you can do.

- ☑ **Certifications are faster & cheaper than college** – Many take **a few months** instead of years.

- ☑ **Work-from-home options** – Many tech jobs allow remote work.

- ☑ **High earning potential** – Top tech fields offer six-figure salaries.

🖊 **How to Get Started:**

- ✔ Take **free or low-cost online courses** (Udemy, Coursera, Google IT Certs).

- ✔ Attend a **coding bootcamp** (3–9 months) for intensive training.

- ✔ Get an **entry-level IT job** and work your way up.

Public Service & First Responder Careers

Public service jobs offer **steady pay, great benefits, and strong pensions.** Many don't require college—just **academy training or certifications.**

🚓 **Examples of Public Service Jobs:**

- ✔ **Firefighter** ($45K–$100K per year)

- ✔ **Police Officer** ($50K–$95K per year)

- ✔ **EMT/Paramedic** ($40K–$75K per year)

- ✔ **Correctional Officer** ($40K–$80K per year)

- ✔ **Postal Service Worker** ($45K–$75K per year)

⚠ **Important Note:** Some government jobs **may** require some college credits, while others do not. **It depends on the jurisdiction.** For example:

- ✔ Some **police departments** require **an associate degree or a certain number of college credits** (but not a full degree).

- ✔ Some **fire departments and correctional agencies** may prefer candidates with **some college coursework** but don't require a full degree.

- ✔ **Federal jobs** often require a degree **or** relevant work experience (meaning you can qualify by working in the field first).

🚀 **How to Get Started:**

- ✔ Apply to a **fire or police academy** (usually a few months of training).

- ✔ Get certified as an **EMT** (3–6 months).

- ✔ Check for **government job openings** in your area.

Medical Careers Without a Degree

Examples of Non-Degree Medical Jobs:

- ✔ **Dental Hygienist** ($60K–$100K per year)

- ✔ **Pharmacy Technician** ($35K–$55K per year)

- ✔ **Ultrasound Technician** ($50K–$90K per year)

- ✔ **Medical Coding & Billing** ($40K–$75K per year)

- ✔ **Phlebotomist (Blood Draw Technician)** ($35K–$55K per year)

High-Value Sales: A High-Paying Job with No Degree Required

💲 **Examples of High-Paying Sales Careers:**

- ✔ **Real Estate Agent** ($50K–$250K+ per year)

- ✔ **B2B Sales (Business-to-Business)** ($60K–$200K per year)

- ✔ **Tech Sales (Software, SaaS, Cybersecurity, etc.)** ($80K–$300K per year)

- ✔ **Financial Services (Insurance, Investments, Mortgage Lending)** ($50K–$200K per year)

- ✔ **Luxury Sales (Cars, Jewelry, High-End Products)** ($50K–$150K per year)

🚀 **How to Get Started:**

- ✔ Consider **real estate or insurance sales**, which often require only a **state license** (no degree).

- ✔ Apply for **entry-level sales jobs** in industries like **tech, logistics, or finance.**

- ✔ Take **sales training courses** online or from industry professionals.

Final Thoughts on Career Options Without College

Skipping college **doesn't** mean settling for a low-paying job. **It means choosing a path that fits you—one where you can build skills, earn well, and succeed without a four-year degree.**

In the next section, we'll explore how you can **build your own career** through **entrepreneurship & freelancing**—because sometimes, the best job is the one you create for yourself.

📖 Section 2: Entrepreneurship and Freelancing

Not everyone wants a traditional 9-to-5 job. Some people thrive when they **work for themselves, set their own schedule, and control their own income.**

The good news? You **don't need a degree** to be your own boss. Whether you're starting a **small business, freelancing, or launching an online brand,** there are countless ways to make money **without working for someone else.**

This section will cover:

- **Entrepreneurship** – Starting your own business

- **Freelancing** – Selling your skills without a traditional job

- **The Pros & Cons** of working for yourself

- **How to get started** with little to no money

Entrepreneurship: Creating Your Own Career

Entrepreneurship is about **building something of your own.** It could be a **physical business, an online store, a service, or a personal brand.** Many of the most successful entrepreneurs started with little more than an idea and the drive to make it work.

🚀 **Examples of Business Ideas You Can Start Without a Degree:**

- **Service-Based Businesses** – Landscaping, home cleaning, pressure washing, personal training, photography

- **Online Stores** – Dropshipping, print-on-demand, handmade crafts (Etsy), flipping products

- **Digital Businesses** – Social media management, consulting, YouTube, blogging, online courses

- **Local & Skilled Trades** – Car detailing, handyman services, mobile car repair, catering

💰 **Why Choose Entrepreneurship?**

✅ **Unlimited earning potential** – You control how much you make.

✅ **Be your own boss** – No one tells you what to do.

✅ **Flexibility** – Work when and where you want.

✅ **Job security** – No one can fire you if you own the business.

⚡ **Reality Check:**

- **It takes time to build success.** Most businesses don't take off overnight.

- **Income isn't guaranteed.** You have to put in the effort to bring in clients/customers.

- **You need to manage everything.** Marketing, finances, and customer service are all on you.

How to Get Started:

- **Pick a business idea** – What can you offer that people will pay for?

- **Start small** – Don't overcomplicate it. Just get your first customers.

- **Market yourself** – Use social media, word of mouth, and local advertising.

- **Learn as you go** – No one has all the answers at the start—just take action!

Freelancing: Getting Paid for Your Skills

Freelancing is a great way to **make money on your own terms** without starting a full business. Instead of working for one employer, you take on **clients and projects** as an independent worker.

Examples of Freelance Work:

- **Writing & Editing** – Articles, blogs, copywriting, resume writing
- **Graphic Design & Branding** – Logos, social media graphics, website design
- **Programming & Tech Services** – Web development, IT support, cybersecurity
- **Photography & Videography** – Events, portraits, social media content
- **Virtual Assistance** – Managing emails, scheduling, customer service
- **Tutoring & Online Teaching** – Test prep, language lessons, skill-based coaching

Why Choose Freelancing?

- **You set your rates** – Charge what you're worth.
- **Choose your clients & projects** – Work on what interests you.
- **Work from anywhere** – Many freelance jobs are remote.
- **Low startup costs** – Most freelance work just requires a laptop and an internet connection.

Reality Check:

- **Freelance income isn't stable at first.** Some months will be busier than others.

- **You have to find your own clients.** No one hands you work— you have to market yourself.

- **No guaranteed benefits.** Unlike traditional jobs, there's no health insurance or retirement plan.

How to Get Started:

Pick a skill – What can you offer that businesses or individuals need?

Set up a portfolio – Show examples of your work (even if they're just practice projects).

Create profiles on freelance websites – Upwork, Fiverr, Free-lancer, etc.

Reach out to potential clients – Send emails, post on social media, and network.

The Pros & Cons of Being Your Own Boss

Pros:

✔ You control your income – No waiting for promotions or pay raises.

✔ Flexible schedule – Work when and where you want.

✔ Creative freedom – Choose what kind of work you do.

✕ Cons:

- ✗ No guaranteed paycheck – You have to find clients/customers.

- ✗ More responsibility – Taxes, marketing, and customer service fall on you.

- ✗ It takes time – Many businesses take months (or even years) to grow.

Low-Cost Ways to Start a Business or Freelance Career

One of the biggest myths about starting your own business is that you need **a lot of money.** That's not true! Many successful businesses and freelance careers started with just **time, effort, and a little creativity.**

Ways to Start Without Much Money:

- **Service-Based Business:** Start with skills you already have (lawn care, tutoring, handyman work, babysitting).

- **Freelancing:** Offer services online (writing, web design, video editing, etc.).

- **Reselling:** Buy and flip items on eBay, Facebook Marketplace, or thrift stores.

- **Content Creation:** Start a YouTube channel, TikTok, or blog to build an audience and monetize later.

If you're **willing to put in the effort,** you can build something from **nothing**—without ever needing a college degree.

Final Thoughts on Entrepreneurship & Freelancing

If you don't want a traditional job, **you don't have to settle.**

If you want **flexibility, freedom, and unlimited earning potential,** working for yourself might be the best path.

It's not always easy, and it takes time, but with the right mindset and effort, you can **create your own career instead of waiting for someone to hire you.**

In the next section, we'll explore **alternative ways to learn and grow your skills without college**—because even if you don't go to school, **education never stops.**

📖 Section 3:
Alternative Learning Paths

Just because you're not going to college **doesn't mean you stop learning.** In fact, **learning is essential** if you want to grow in your career, start a business, or move into higher-paying roles.

The difference? **You don't have to spend four years and thousands of dollars to do it.**

There are **plenty of ways to gain valuable skills and certifications** without taking on college debt. In this section, we'll explore:

- **Apprenticeships & Trade Schools** – Hands-on learning with real-world experience
- **Employer-Paid Training Programs** – Companies that will pay you to learn
- **Industry Certifications** – Credentials that boost your job opportunities
- **Self-Directed Learning** – Free and low-cost ways to gain high-value skills

Apprenticeships & Trade Schools: Learn by Doing

Apprenticeships and trade schools offer **structured, hands-on training** that leads directly to jobs. Instead of sitting in a lecture hall, you **learn by working in the field**—and often **get paid while doing it.**

🔧 **Examples of Careers with Apprenticeships or Trade Schools:**

- **Electrician** (Apprenticeship required)

- **Plumber** (Apprenticeship required)

- **HVAC Technician** (Trade school or apprenticeship)

- **Carpenter** (Trade school or apprenticeship)

- **Welding** (Trade school certification)

- **Automotive Technician** (Trade school or on-the-job training)

💰 **Why Choose This Path?**

☑ **Fast track to a career** – Most programs last 6 months to 2 years.

☑ **Earn while you learn** – Many apprenticeships **pay you** while you train.

☑ **High job demand** – Skilled trades are always needed.

☑ **No massive student debt** – Apprenticeships are free or low-cost, and trade school is much cheaper than college.

🪶 How to Get Started:

- Search for **registered apprenticeships** on sites like **apprenticeship.gov** (U.S.) or check local trade unions.

- Look for **local trade schools** that offer certifications in high-demand fields.

- Contact companies in the field and ask if they offer **on-the-job training programs.**

Employer-Paid Training Programs

Some companies **train you for free** as long as you agree to work for them after. This is a great option if you want to **learn a skill without paying for school.**

💼 Examples of Jobs with Paid Training:

- ✔ Commercial Trucking (CDL) – Some trucking companies cover your CDL training.

- ✔ IT & Tech Companies – Many large tech firms offer training for cybersecurity, networking, and IT support.

- ✔ Healthcare – Some hospitals train medical assistants, phlebotomists, or patient care techs.

- ✔ Manufacturing & Skilled Labor – Some companies train machinists, welders, or factory workers from scratch.

🪶 How to Get Started:

- ✔ Look up **"paid training jobs"** on job boards like **Indeed** or **LinkedIn**.

- ✔ Check **company websites** for workforce development programs.

✔ Call local **hospitals, manufacturing plants, or transportation companies** and ask about training opportunities.

Industry Certifications: A Fast, Affordable Way to Prove Your Skills

Industry certifications can **replace a degree in many fields.** These credentials show employers that you **know your stuff—**without spending four years in school.

Examples of In-Demand Certifications:

- **IT & Cybersecurity:** Google IT Support, CompTIA A+, Cisco CCNA, AWS Cloud

- **Project Management & Business:** PMP, Scrum Master, Six Sigma

- **Digital Marketing & E-Commerce:** Google Analytics, Hub-Spot, Facebook Blueprint

- **Medical & Healthcare:** Certified Medical Assistant, Phlebotomy Technician

- **Skilled Trades:** OSHA Safety, HVAC, Electrical Journeyman

Why Choose This Path?

- **Faster & cheaper than a degree** – Most certifications take **weeks or months, not years.**

- **Boosts job opportunities** – Many employers prefer certified candidates.

- **Helps you switch careers** – Great if you want to move into a new industry.

How to Get Started:

- Search for **certifications in your industry** (many are offered online).

- Look at company job postings to see **which certifications they prefer.**

- Enroll in online courses on sites like **Coursera, Udemy, LinkedIn Learning.**

Self-Directed Learning: Teach Yourself High-Paying Skills

Some of the most successful people **never set foot in a classroom** after high school. Instead, they **taught themselves skills and built careers from scratch.**

Ways to Learn on Your Own:

- **Online Courses & Bootcamps** – Udemy, Coursera, Skillshare, YouTube tutorials

- **Books & Audiobooks** – Read about business, sales, marketing, tech, or entrepreneurship

- **Internships & Volunteering** – Gain real-world experience for free

- **Building Your Own Projects** – If you want to be a **writer, designer, coder, or content creator**, start practicing and **create your own portfolio**

Why Choose This Path?

- **No cost (or very low cost)** – Many resources are free or cheap.

- **Learn at your own pace** – No schedules, no deadlines.

- **Perfect for tech, creative, and business fields** – Many careers (like web development, graphic design, and social media marketing) don't require formal education—just skills.

How to Get Started:

- ✔ Pick **one skill** you want to learn.

- ✔ Find **free or cheap online courses.**

- ✔ Set a **weekly goal** for practice.

✔ Apply what you learn by **creating something real.**

Final Thoughts on Alternative Learning Paths

Skipping college **doesn't mean you stop learning.** It just means you're learning **in a smarter, faster, and more affordable way.**

Whether it's through **apprenticeships, certifications, online courses, or employer training,** you have **plenty of options** to build a great career without drowning in student debt.

In the next section, we'll cover **how to actually get hired without a degree**—because knowing the skills is one thing, but **proving your value to employers is what lands you the job.**

📖 Section 4: Getting Hired Without a Degree

You have the skills. You've learned the trade, earned the certifications, or built a solid freelancing portfolio. Now, you just need one thing: **a job.**

The good news? **A degree is just one way to prove you're qualified—** but it's not the only way. Many employers care **more about what you can do** than a piece of paper saying you went to school.

This section will cover:

   ✓ **How to stand out on a résumé without a degree**

   ✓ **How to use networking to get hired faster**

   ✓ **How to ace interviews and prove your value**

   ✓ **How to negotiate pay and benefits**

📑 How to Stand Out on a Résumé Without a Degree

Most people think their résumé has to start with 'Education.' **Not you.**

When you don't have a degree, **you highlight skills, experience, and results first.**

How to Format Your Résumé:

✓ **Skip the "Education" section** (or move it to the bottom).

✓ **Start with a strong 'Skills' section** – Highlight what you can actually do.

✓ **Use a 'Projects' or 'Certifications' section** – Show proof of your work.

✓ **List experience creatively** – If you don't have formal work experience, include freelance work, apprenticeships, internships, or personal projects.

👥 How to Use Networking to Get Hired Faster

Most jobs **aren't even listed online—they're filled through word of mouth.** That's why networking is **so important.**

How to Network Like a Pro:

✓ **Talk to people in your industry.** Join **Facebook Groups, LinkedIn groups, or Reddit forums** in your field.

✓ **Attend local events & meetups.** Look for **career nights, job fairs, or industry networking events.**

✓ **Reach out directly.** Message hiring managers or business owners and ask for advice instead of just asking for a job.

✎ How to Ace an Interview (Without a Degree)

Once you land an interview, **your job is to prove you can do the work.**

Interview Tips for Non-Degree Candidates:

✓ **Be confident** – Show employers that you are skilled and capable.

✓ **Show proof of your abilities** – Bring a portfolio, project samples, or certification documents.

✓ **Turn experience into results** – Instead of saying, "I worked on social media," say, "I helped a local brand grow from 500 to 5,000 followers in 3 months."

§ How to Negotiate Pay & Benefits (Even Without a Degree)

Many employers **offer lower pay** to non-degree candidates—**unless you negotiate.**

How to Get Paid What You're Worth:

✓ **Do your research** – Look up average salaries on sites like **Glassdoor and Payscale.**

✓ **Talk about your results** – Employers pay for **value, not degrees.**

✓ **Be willing to ask** – Most employers **expect candidates to negotiate.**

Final Thoughts on Getting Hired Without a Degree

A degree is just one way to get a job—it's not the only way.

✓ If you have **skills, proof of work, and confidence,** you can land a great job.

✓ **Networking and hands-on experience matter more than a diploma.**

✓ **The best way to prove yourself is to show what you can do.**

In the next section, we'll explore **how to choose a career that's built to last—so you don't waste time in a job that disappears in 5 years.**

📖 Section 5: Future-Proof Careers and Industry Trends

The job market is always changing. New industries emerge, technology advances, and some jobs **disappear completely.**

If you're skipping college, you want to make sure you're not stepping into a **dead-end job.** You need a **future-proof career**—one that will stay in demand and **continue to grow** in the coming years.

This section will cover:

- [ ] **What makes a career future-proof?**
- [ ] **Industries that are growing fast**
- [ ] **Jobs that won't be replaced by AI or automation**
- [ ] **How to choose a career that lasts**

What Makes a Career Future-Proof?

A **future-proof job** is one that is:

✓ **In high demand** – Companies are actively hiring and struggling to find workers.

✓ **Not easily replaced by AI or robots** – Jobs that require human creativity, adaptability, or hands-on work are safer.

✓ **Flexible & evolving** – Jobs that allow you to learn new skills and shift as industries change.

🖊 **Examples of Careers at Risk of Automation:**

- ✕ Data entry clerks (AI can do it faster)
- ✕ Retail cashiers (Self-checkouts are replacing them)
- ✕ Some customer service roles (AI chatbots are taking over)
- ✕ Basic administrative assistants (Automated scheduling & AI tools are improving)

Industries That Are Growing Fast

These fields are **expanding rapidly** and offer **strong job security** for years to come.

Skilled Trades & Infrastructure Jobs

Why It's Future-Proof: Skilled labor is always needed, and most of these jobs **can't be automated.**

High-Demand Trades:

- **Electricians** ($50K–$90K per year)
- **Plumbers** ($50K–$100K per year)
- **Welders** ($40K–$85K per year)
- **HVAC Technicians** ($45K–$80K per year)
- **Heavy Equipment Operators** ($50K–$95K per year)

Why Choose This Path?

- These jobs are essential—**people always need heating, plumbing, and electricity.**
- They **can't be outsourced**—someone has to do the work locally.
- Demand is growing as **older tradespeople retire.**

Tech & Cybersecurity

Why It's Future-Proof: Tech is evolving **faster than ever,** and companies need skilled workers to **protect their data and systems.**

In-Demand Tech Jobs (No Degree Required):

- **IT Support Specialist** ($40K–$75K per year)

- **Cybersecurity Analyst** ($60K–$120K per year)

- **Cloud Computing Specialist** ($70K–$150K per year)

- **Data Analyst** ($55K–$110K per year)

- **Software Tester** ($50K–$100K per year)

Why Choose This Path?

- Many tech jobs **focus on skills, not degrees.**

- **Certifications** can replace a degree and get you hired faster.

- Cybersecurity & cloud computing jobs are growing **at twice the national average.**

3 Healthcare & Medical Support Jobs

Why It's Future-Proof: People will **always** need medical care. As the population ages, demand for healthcare workers is skyrocketing.

In-Demand Medical Jobs Without a Degree:

- **Dental Hygienist** ($60K–$100K per year)

- **Medical Assistant** ($40K–$65K per year)

- **Ultrasound Technician** ($50K–$90K per year)

- **Pharmacy Technician** ($35K–$55K per year)

- **Phlebotomist (Blood Draw Technician)** ($35K–$55K per year)

Why Choose This Path?

- Many healthcare jobs require **only certifications or a 1-2 year training program.**

- **Medical careers offer stability,** with thousands of job openings every year.

- Demand is **growing fast** as people live longer and need more healthcare services.

Green Energy & Environmental Careers

Why It's Future-Proof: As the world shifts to **renewable energy**, careers in solar, wind, and energy efficiency are booming.

High-Demand Green Jobs:

- **Solar Panel Installer** ($45K–$80K per year)

- **Wind Turbine Technician** ($50K–$100K per year)

- **Environmental Technician** ($40K–$80K per year)

- **Energy Efficiency Auditor** ($50K–$90K per year)

Why Choose This Path?

- The **renewable energy industry is growing rapidly.**

- Governments and companies are investing **billions** in green energy.

- Many positions require **only short-term training or apprenticeships.**

5 High-Value Sales & Business Development

Why It's Future-Proof: As long as companies **need to make money,** they'll need salespeople to **bring in revenue.**

High-Paying Sales Careers (No Degree Required):

- **Real Estate Agent** ($50K–$250K+ per year)

- **B2B Sales (Business-to-Business)** ($60K–$200K per year)

- **Tech Sales (Software, SaaS, Cybersecurity, etc.)** ($80K–$300K per year)

- **Financial Services (Insurance, Investments, Mortgage Lending)** ($50K–$200K per year)

- **Luxury Sales (Cars, Jewelry, High-End Products)** ($50K–$150K per year)

Why Choose This Path?

- Sales careers have **unlimited earning potential** with commission-based pay.

- **No degree required**—companies care about **results, not diplomas.**

- It teaches **transferable skills** (communication, persuasion, negotiation).

How to Choose a Career That Lasts

If you want job security **without a degree,** follow these **four steps:**

Step 1: Pick an industry that's growing.

> 🔍 Look for **job growth projections** on sites like the **Bureau of Labor Statistics (BLS).**

Step 2: Choose a job that can't be automated.

> 🤖 Avoid jobs that could be replaced by AI or machines.

Step 3: Find a skill that's in demand.

> 📄 If companies **struggle to hire** for a role, it means there's **high demand** and **great pay.**

Step 4: Keep learning & adapting.

> 🎓 Take **online courses, certifications, or apprenticeships** to **stay ahead of changes** in your industry.

Final Thoughts on Future-Proof Careers

Choosing a **future-proof career** means picking a job that will **still exist, grow, and pay well in the years ahead.**

> The best jobs without a degree **focus on skills, experience, and adaptability.**

In the next section, we'll talk about **money—how skipping college can set you up for financial success early on.**

📖 Section 6:
The Financial Advantages
of Skipping or Delaying College

One of the biggest benefits of skipping or delaying college is **financial freedom.**

While many people think of a college degree as a "safe investment," the reality is that **student debt, lost earning years, and high tuition costs** can put people at a financial disadvantage for decades.

This section will cover:

- The cost of college vs. earning earlier
- How skipping student loans gives you a financial head start
- The power of investing early
- How delaying college can be a smarter choice

The True Cost of College vs. Starting Work Earlier

Many students go to college because they're told it's the **"smart financial choice."** But let's break down the **real numbers.**

Average Cost of College (4-Year Degree)

- **Public University (In-State):** $25,000–$35,000 per year ($100K–$140K total)
- **Private University:** $40,000–$60,000 per year ($160K–$240K total)
- **Lost Earnings While in School:** ~$30,000 per year (if you're not working full-time)
- **Student Loan Interest:** Adds $10K–$50K+ in extra costs over time

Total Estimated Cost of a College Degree: $150,000–$300,000+

Now, Compare That to Starting a Job or Trade at 18:

- **Earn $40K–$60K per year right away**
- **Gain 4 years of real work experience**
- **Invest and save money instead of taking on debt**

The Bottom Line:

A 22-year-old with a college degree often has **$50K+ in student debt** and **no work experience.**

A 22-year-old who started working at 18 could have **$100K+ in earnings, work experience, and no debt.**

Which sounds like a better financial head start?

The Power of Avoiding Student Loan Debt

🎓 **How Much Do Student Loans Actually Cost You?**

Let's say you take out **$50,000 in student loans** at a **6% interest rate.**

- **Monthly Payment:** ~$550 per month
- **Time to Pay Off: 10–20 years**
- **Total Interest Paid: $10K–$30K+**

That's **hundreds of dollars a month** that could be going toward **a house, a car, or investments instead of loan payments.**

What Could You Do Without Student Loan Debt?

Save for a house sooner

Invest in retirement early

Start your own business

Have more financial freedom in your 20s and 30s

The Power of Investing Early

📈 **How Much Can Early Investing Grow?**

Let's compare **someone who skips college and starts investing at 18** vs. **someone who goes to college and starts investing at 22.**

Person A (No College, Starts Investing at 18)

- Invests just **$300 per month**
- **7% average annual return**
- **At age 40: $350,000+**

Person B (Goes to College, Starts Investing at 22)

- Invests the same **$300 per month**
- **Same 7% return**
- **At age 40: $250,000+**

Why This Matters:

The person who **started investing at 18** has **$100,000 more** just because they started **four years earlier.**

This is the **power of compound interest**—your money makes money **faster when you start sooner.**

Delaying College: A Smarter Alternative

Not sure if college is the right choice? You can always go later.

One of the biggest **misconceptions** is that you have to **go to college right after high school—or not at all.** That's **not true.**

🎯 **Reasons to Delay College:**

✓ Try out different jobs before committing to a degree.

✓ Save money and pay for college **without student loans.**

✓ Build work experience that makes you more valuable to employers.

✓ Avoid wasting time (and money) on a degree you're not sure about.

📚 **How to Make College More Affordable Later:**

- Work for a company that **offers tuition reimbursement.**

- Attend community college first, then transfer.

- Pay cash for classes while working, instead of taking out loans.

🚀 The Bottom Line:

Not choosing college **right now** doesn't mean you're saying no forever. It just means you're choosing a **smarter, more affordable path.**

Final Thoughts on the Financial Benefits of Skipping or Delaying College

Skipping college (or delaying it) gives you:

✓ **A massive financial head start** (no debt + early income)

✓ **More career flexibility** (you're not tied to one degree)

✓ **The ability to invest early and build wealth faster**

In the next section, we'll talk about **how to keep growing your career long-term—so you're not just getting a job, but building a future.**

📖 Section 7:
Career Growth and Long-Term Success Without a Degree

Getting your first job is just the beginning. The real key to **long-term success** is knowing **how to grow, adapt, and move up**—even without a degree.

This section will cover:

✅ **How to build a career roadmap** (set goals and level up)

✅ **The best ways to gain promotions and raises**

✅ **Certifications and training for career advancement**

✅ **How to pivot into higher-paying jobs over time**

Building Your Career Roadmap

A lot of people just **take a job and hope for the best.** But the people who grow into **high-paying, fulfilling careers** usually **plan ahead.**

🔍 **How to Create a Career Roadmap:**

1️⃣ **Pick a General Direction** – What industry do you want to be in? (Tech, skilled trades, sales, healthcare, etc.)

2️⃣ **Set a 1-Year Goal** – What's the next level? (Getting a promotion, learning a new skill, increasing income)

3️⃣ **Set a 5-Year Goal** – Where do you want to be? (Manager, business owner, top-level expert in your field)

4️⃣ **Identify Skills You Need** – What training or experience will help you move up?

🚀 Example Career Roadmap:

- **Start:** Entry-level IT Support job ($40K)

- **Year 1 Goal:** Earn Google IT Certification

- **Year 2 Goal:** Get promoted to Network Administrator ($60K)

- **Year 5 Goal:** Move into Cybersecurity ($90K+)

🎯 Why This Works:

✓ Instead of drifting from job to job, you're **working toward something bigger.**

✓ You know **what skills to focus on** to move up faster.

✓ Employers see you as **driven and goal-oriented**, which makes them invest in you.

How to Get Promotions & Pay Raises Without a Degree

✏️ **Want to move up faster? Here's how:**

📋 **1. Be the person who solves problems.**

- The best way to get promoted? **Make your boss's job easier.**
- Take initiative, suggest improvements, and go the extra mile.

📋 **2. Learn skills that make you more valuable.**

- If you're in **tech**, get a new certification.
- If you're in **trades**, master a specialty (like solar for electricians).
- If you're in **sales**, take a negotiation or leadership course.

📋 **3. Ask for more responsibility (then prove yourself).**

- Volunteer to lead projects.
- Help train new employees.
- Show that you're **already doing the next job before you get the title.**

📋 **4. Document your wins.**

- Keep track of how you've **helped the company.**
- Did you **save them money? Increase sales? Improve efficiency?**
- When it's time for a raise, **you have proof of your value.**

✅ 5. Negotiate your salary.

- Research industry pay rates.
- Show why you deserve a raise based on **results, not just time served.**
- If they can't give you a raise, **ask for new responsibilities or career growth opportunities.**

Certifications & Training for Career Advancement

Even if you don't have a degree, **certifications, online courses, and specialized training** can help you move up fast.

Examples of Certifications for Career Growth:

💻 Tech & IT:

- CompTIA Security+ (Cybersecurity)
- AWS Cloud Practitioner (Cloud Computing)
- Google Data Analytics

✕ Skilled Trades:

- Master Electrician License

- HVAC Specialties (Geothermal, Refrigeration, etc.)

- OSHA Safety Certifications

Business & Sales:

- HubSpot Sales Certification

- Dale Carnegie Sales Training

- Google Ads & Facebook Ads Certifications

Healthcare:

- Advanced EMT Training

- Pharmacy Technician Certification

- Medical Coding & Billing

How to Find the Best Certifications for Your Career:

- Check job listings to see **what certifications employers prefer.**

- Ask people in your field **which ones helped them get promoted.**

- Look for online programs that offer **flexible, affordable training.**

How to Pivot Into Higher-Paying Jobs Over Time

Your first job **doesn't have to be your forever job.** Many people **start in one field** and **use their skills to move into a higher-paying career.**

🚀 **How to Pivot to a Better Job:**

☑ **1. Identify Transferable Skills.**

- If you're in **customer service**, you already have **sales & communication skills.**

- If you're in **retail**, you have **inventory, management, and business skills.**

- If you're in **a trade**, you might be able to **start your own business.**

☑ **2. Gain Experience While Working.**

- Want to switch into **tech?** Get an entry-level IT certification while still working your current job.

- Want to move into **management?** Ask for leadership responsibilities where you are now.

- Want to start your own business? **Build it as a side hustle first.**

☑ **3. Network with People in Your Target Industry.**

- Connect with people on **LinkedIn, at industry events, or through online communities.**

- Learn from those who have **already made the switch.**

✎ **Example Career Pivots:**

- 🔹 **Retail Sales → Tech Sales → Software Sales ($150K+)**

- 🔹 **Warehouse Worker → Logistics Coordinator → Supply Chain Manager ($100K+)**

- 🔹 **Plumber → Plumbing Business Owner ($200K+)**

- 🔹 **Freelance Graphic Designer → Marketing Director ($120K+)**

A Note About Career Ceilings Without a Degree

As you move up in your career, you might find that some industries or companies **require a degree for higher-level management positions.** This isn't always the case, but it's something to be **aware of as you plan your long-term goals.**

- ✓ Many companies **care more about experience than degrees,** but in some fields, having a diploma **may be required for leadership roles.**

- ✓ If you ever hit a ceiling, **there are workarounds—such as getting industry certifications, attending leadership training, or even pursuing a degree later on** (many companies offer tuition reimbursement).

- ✓ The key is to **know your industry and plan ahead** so you're never caught off guard.

✎ **Bottom Line:**

Not having a degree **won't stop you from building a successful career**, but knowing where limitations **might** appear helps you **prepare in advance** and stay in control of your growth.

Final Thoughts on Career Growth Without a Degree

A degree isn't what gets you promoted—your skills, work ethic, and mindset do.

✓ **Plan your career growth** like a roadmap, not just a series of random jobs.

✓ **Continuously build new skills** through certifications and hands-on learning.

✓ **Look for ways to add value** and make yourself indispensable to your company.

✓ **Be ready to pivot** into higher-paying roles as new opportunities arise.

📖 Final Thoughts and Action Steps

By now, you've seen that **a successful career without college is 100% possible**—but it doesn't just happen on its own.

Skipping college **doesn't mean less work.** It means **a different kind of work.**

Instead of spending four years in a classroom, you'll be:

- Learning through hands-on experience
- Earning certifications or industry-specific training
- Building a portfolio or proving your skills in real-world settings
- Networking and seeking out opportunities to advance

The path to success **without college** is about **taking control of your own career, continuously improving, and staying adaptable.** If you do that, you can **achieve just as much—if not more—than someone with a degree.**

What to Do Next: Your Action Plan

🚀 **Step 1: Choose Your Career Path**

- Do you want to work in **skilled trades, tech, healthcare, sales, or entrepreneurship?**

- Research what industries **interest you the most.**

🚀 **Step 2: Learn the Skills You Need**

- Look into **apprenticeships, certifications, or self-paced learning.**

- Find free or low-cost training options (**YouTube, Udemy, Coursera, Google, trade schools**).

🚀 **Step 3: Get Experience & Start Earning**

- Apply for **entry-level jobs or internships** in your chosen field.

- Offer **freelance or part-time services** to build your resume and skills.

- Join **networking groups, LinkedIn, and industry events** to connect with professionals.

Step 4: Keep Learning & Growing

- Take **higher-level certifications or training** as you advance.

- Look for **mentorship opportunities** from experienced professionals.

- Set **career goals** and keep pushing toward the next level.

A Final Word: Your Future Is in Your Hands

Skipping college **doesn't close doors—it opens different ones.**

But to succeed, **you have to be willing to put in the work.**

> It's not about taking an "easier" route—it's about taking the route that fits YOU best.

✓ If you stay **focused, proactive, and always learning**, you can build a **stable, high-paying, and fulfilling career**—without ever setting foot in a college classroom.

The opportunities are out there. **Go get them.**

About the Author

Jennifer Larsen has a habit of turning big questions into clear, doable steps—and she's built a career around helping others do the same. With a background in education and psychology (and a low tolerance for boring advice), she has created this guide for anyone tired of being asked, "What do you want to be when you grow up?"—especially if they're already grown.

More from the "Can't I Just..." Series

Can't I Just Stay in My Room?

A Career Guidebook for Those Who Would Rather Not Talk About It

If you're overwhelmed, stuck, or just tired of being asked what you're doing with your life—this book is your startWith a conversational tone and practical, kind advice, this guide walks readers through the messy in-between s"More helpful than most school career days ever were."
—G.M. Theroux

"The best value in the career space—
especially compared to coaching or college."
—Mike Lazarus

"Warm, practical, and exactly what overwhelmed teens need."
—Peter Jay Gould

"An easy, non-preachy way to start conversations about the future."
—Phyfed

Available now in paperback, Kindle, and audiobook on Amazon.

Follow the series and find more at cantijust.com or on Instagram: @cantijustbooks

More titles in the "Can't I Just..." series coming soon!

www.ingramcontent.com/pod-product-compliance
Lightning Source LLC
Chambersburg PA
CBHW070350130626
46556CB00007B/3118